A BILINGUAL BOOK IN ENGLISH AND

Wassily

Wassily Kandinsky is a very famous artist.

Wassily Kandinsky es un artista muy famoso.

Wassily Kandinsky was born on December 16, 1866, in Moscow, Russia. He grew up in a city named Odessa

map - mapa

Wassily Kandinsky nació el 16 de diciembre de 1866 en Moscú, Rusia. Creció en una ciudad llamada Odessa.

As a child he loved music and played the cello and the piano. He also loved to draw and paint.

De niño le gustaba la música y tocaba el violonchelo y el piano. También le gustaba dibujar y pintar.

Colors were very important to him. He had a special gift where he could hear certain sounds when he saw certain colors. It was like he was combining two of his senses into one, both sight and hearing.

Los colores eran muy importantes para él. Tenía un don especial por el que podía oír ciertos sonidos cuando veía ciertos colores. Era como si combinara dos de sus sentidos en uno, la vista y el oído.

This special talent is called synesthesia. Some people can combine or mix up two senses. That was a pretty amazing talent, so his father made sure he had music lessons and art lessons.

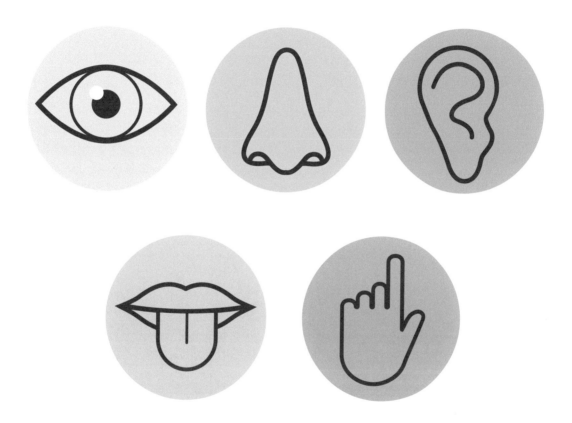

Este talento especial se llama sinestesia. Algunas personas pueden combinar o mezclar dos sentidos. Era un talento sorprendente, así que su padre se aseguró de que recibiera clases de música y de arte.

From 1886 and 1892 Kandinsky went to college to become a lawyer and a teacher. In 1893 he became a law professor at the University of Moscow.

Entre 1886 y 1892, Kandinsky fue a la universidad para convertirse en abogado y profesor. En 1893 se convirtió en profesor de derecho en la Universidad de Moscú.

However, he missed art and music very much. When he was thirty years old he left his job to become an artist. He moved to Munich, Germany, and enrolled in art school.

Sin embargo, echaba mucho de menos el arte y la música. A los treinta años dejó su trabajo para convertirse en artista. Se trasladó a Múnich (Alemania) y se matriculó en una escuela de arte.

Kandinsky liked the style of impressionist artists who used color and light to paint. In 1903 he was painting landscapes and figures.

A Kandinsky le gustaba el estilo de los artistas impresionistas que utilizaban el color y la luz para pintar. En 1903 pintaba paisajes y figuras.

However, color was more important than the details of a painting. His paintings started to become more about color than about figures.

Sin embargo, el color era más importante que los detalles de un cuadro. Sus cuadros empezaron a centrarse más en el color que en las figuras.

He painted things that were real and things that were not. Colors and shapes were used to show feelings.

Pintaba cosas que eran reales y cosas que no lo eran. Los colores y las formas se utilizaban para mostrar sentimientos.

By 1913, Kandinsky was painting abstract figures, shapes, and lines. His paintings were inspired by music.

En 1913, Kandinsky ya pintaba figuras, formas y líneas abstractas. Sus cuadros se inspiran en la música.

He named many of his paintings "Compositions" with Roman Numerals as if they were musical sounds and songs.

Llamó a muchos de ellos Composiciones con números romanos, como si fueran sonidos y canciones musicales.

Roman Numerals

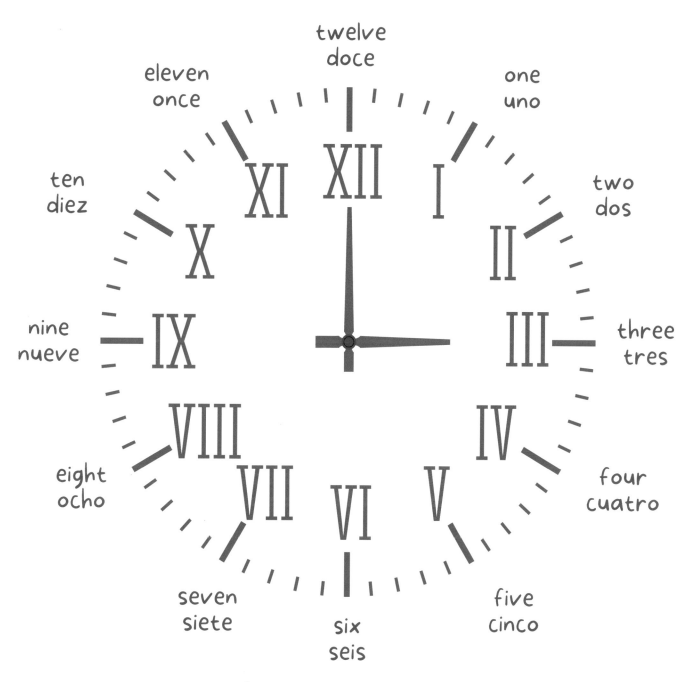

twelve
doce

eleven
once

one
uno

ten
diez

two
dos

nine
nueve

three
tres

eight
ocho

four
cuatro

seven
siete

five
cinco

six
seis

Números romanos

Remember, he had a special talent that combined what he saw with what he heard. This helped develop into his own unique style of painting.

Recuerda que tenía un talento especial que combinaba lo que veía con lo que oía. Esto le ayudó a desarrollar su propio y único estilo de pintura.

Later between 1922 and 1933, he began to add geometric shapes to his paintings. Most of his paintings now included triangles, lines, curves, and circles.

Más tarde, entre 1922 y 1933, empezó a añadir formas geométricas a sus cuadros. La mayoría de sus cuadros incluían ahora triángulos, líneas, curvas y círculos.

Shapes

circle
el circulo

square
el cuadrado

hexagon
el hexágono

triangle
el triángulo

rectangle
el rectángulo

rhombus
el rombo

oval
el óvalo

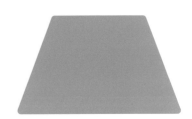

trapezoid
el trapezoide

Las formas

He expressed feelings through shapes. He thought triangles were angry and squares were peaceful.

Expresaba sus sentimientos a través de las formas. Pensaba que los triángulos eran de ira y los cuadrados de paz.

It is very easy to recognize one of his paintings because there are so many shapes. He became one of the world's greatest abstract artists.

Es muy fácil reconocer uno de sus cuadros porque hay muchas formas. Se convirtió en uno de los mayores artistas abstractos del mundo.

In 1933, Kandinsky moved to France with his wife. He had an art studio in Neuilly-sur-Seine, France. He lived there until he died on December 13, 1944.

En 1933, Kandinsky se trasladó a Francia con su mujer. Tenía un estudio de arte en Neuilly-sur-Seine, Francia. Murió el 13 de diciembre de 1944.

He is thought to be one of the first real abstract artists.

Se le considera uno de los primeros artistas abstractos de verdad.

Many abstract artists learned from him and began to create abstract paintings. His original style influenced many artists who came after him.

Muchos artistas abstractos aprendieron de él y empezaron a crear cuadros abstractos. Su original estilo influyó en muchos artistas que vinieron después.

KANDINSKY
HEARTS

Step by Step

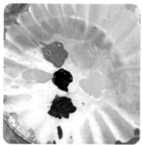

Choose the paint colors for your project. You will need a brush and a small cup of water.

Fold paper into 6 sections. Trace a heart into one of the boxes.

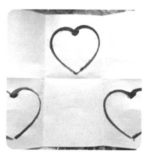

Continue to trace 1 heart into each section.

Paint a thin heart inside each heart using a different color.

Continue painting hearts inside hearts using different colors.

Be careful so the colors do not overlap too much.

The hearts look best with many different colors.

Keep painting hearts inside hearts until they are filled.

Great! Step 1 is complete!

Step by Step

Choose 6 different colors to paint the background the hearts.

Carefully paint around each heart.

Almost done. Looking good!

All done!

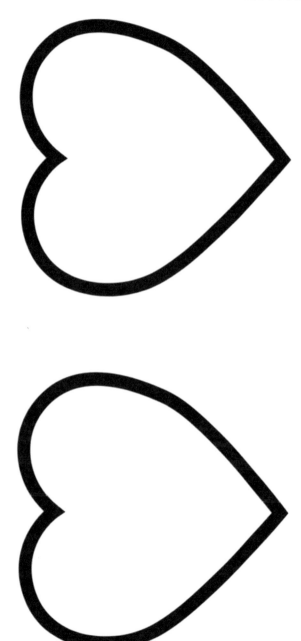

PAINTINGS

Explore More Bilingual Books

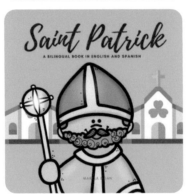

MAGICSPELLSFORTEACHERS.COM

Available at
amazon

Art Activity Workbooks

Available at